OCEAN OF FLOWERS

POEMS & KOANS

mark h fitzpatrick

for
Grady

I love you
more than
love

ISBN: 978-1-9992873-3-7

First edition: October 2020

Thank you to the artists that helped bring this book to life.

Cover and title page art for Shin Tattoos,
Strange Birds, and Silver Dishes by Jorm Sangsorn.

Interior graphic art by Grandfailure and Grandeduc.

Photography by:

Anastasia Dulgier   Jilbert Ebrahimi   Pratik Patel
Anton Angelgardt   Jong Marshes   Quang Le
Anyana Wyse   Josiah Weiss   Raphael Stäger
Aziz Ayad   Jovis Aloor
Beckett Ruiz   K. Mitch Hodge
Bruno Kelzer   Kristopher Roller
Chandan Chaurasia   Lucie Dawson
Chris Stenger   Marc-Olivier Jodoin   Reza Hasannia
Crisserbug   Marc Sendra Martorell Sea Change Canada
David Babayan   Max LaRochelle   Sharon McCutcheon
David Becker   Mel Poole   Skeeze
Dirkr   Nadiya Ploschenko   Sofia Sforza
Inga Gezalian   Olivier Collet   Timothy Eberly
Jeremy Bishop   Owen Spencer   Thulasi Nakkeeran
Jessica Wong   Patrick Tomasso   Tolga Ahmetler

All images courtesy of iStock/Getty, Pixabay, and Unsplash.

poems
& koans

Ocean of Flowers

mark h fitzpatrick

SHIN TATTOOS

KOANS

STRANGE BIRDS

MORE KOANS

SILVER DISHES

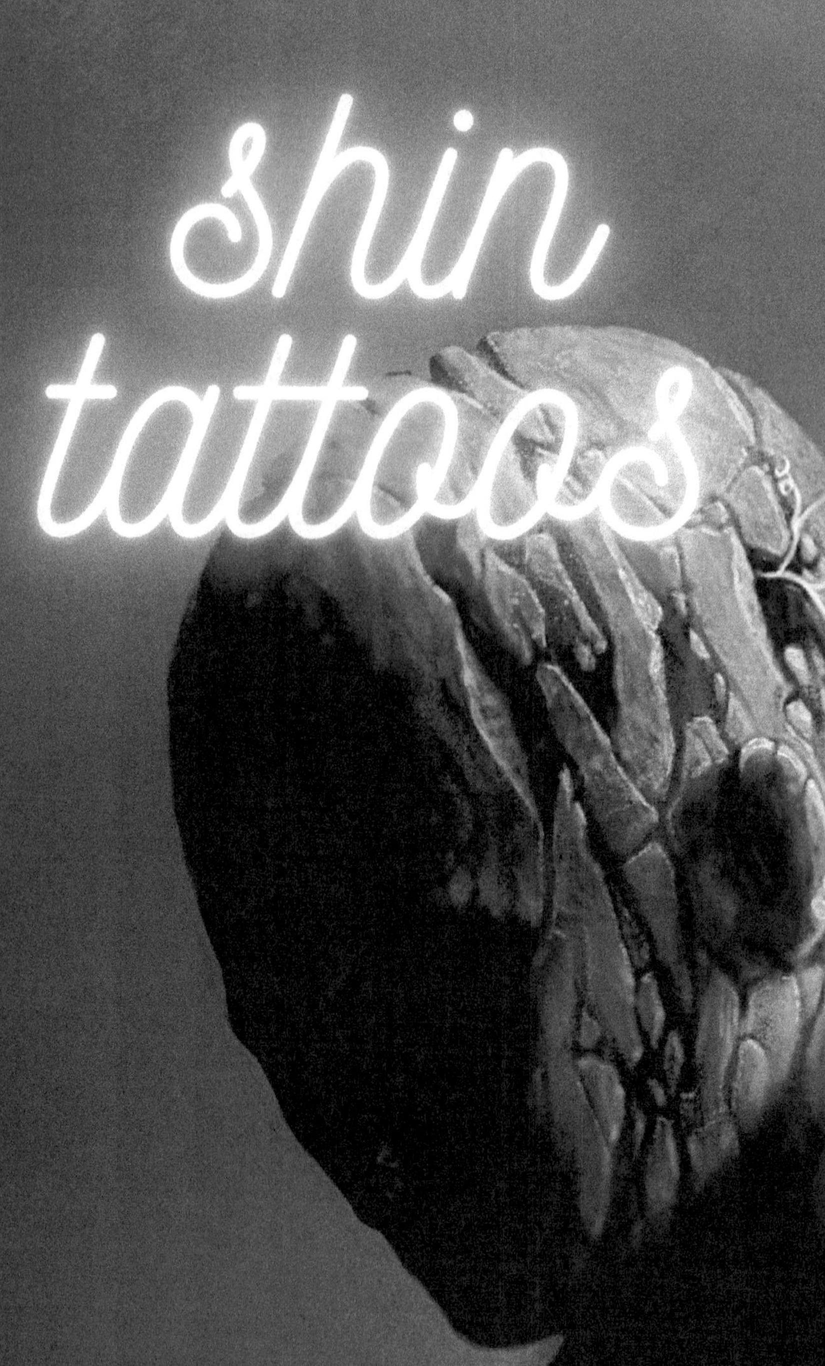
shin
tattoos

&
other poems
that hurt
so good

shin tattoos

I once lived
in black & white
NY arcades
& youth drunk on
the sped-upness
of cigarettes
& tattoo guns
gunning shins

what else to do
with a universe
burrowing under
my skin

but then I heard
poets say if each
contains multitudes
it just takes two
to tip the scales

truce

careless arrow's refuge
fire filled with stones
swift kick to perception
entrails silvered gold

thought born of another
feeling put to use
confusion is the danger
lilies whisper truce

feet of clay squeeze wetness
sorrow cured by sight
flashing dewdrops end me
melting into light

cardinal

I am the rug beneath
which there is no floor

the sun's violence
on fragrant throats
& hollow bones

an island of color
slicing through
your emergency

the heat of your anger
the fire of your heart

just a bird

more orange than you think,
as red as you believe

crisis

the meaning of dreams
watches us sleep as we
chase the finality of
apartments silent but for
the creak of our skin
saying darkness can
never be whole

(violated as it is by
the seed of light
that runs through
our bodies)

so lower the knife,

let no good crisis
go to waste

treehouse

in a treehouse
above the boneyard
sleeps a hero
fighting through
midnight-markets
& outland sprawl
but the setting
collapses under
weight of its
fictions leaving
the boy stranded
in vast systems
of untravelled
bike paths where
life unfolds at
a different speed

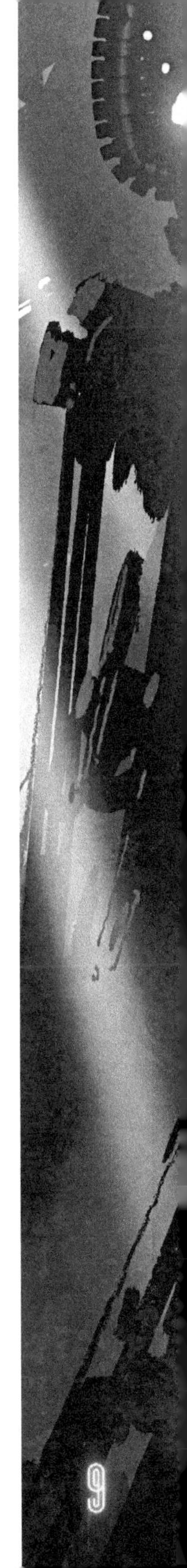

naked

sparrows sleep
& ermines slip
quiet as cats
through neon
blooms pulsing
like the echo
of our need
to know:

what animates these
pagodas of bone?

the dawn slithers

& in a burst
of red
I am found

naked behind
these words

hyphen

the gravestone dash
is a ronin sword
of orgasm & rage

a life of skies
rose-fingered
& gray

tempered by
poems unread
& those never
read again

a hyphen slicing
infant cry from
dying thought

our last kiss

fading with
the weather

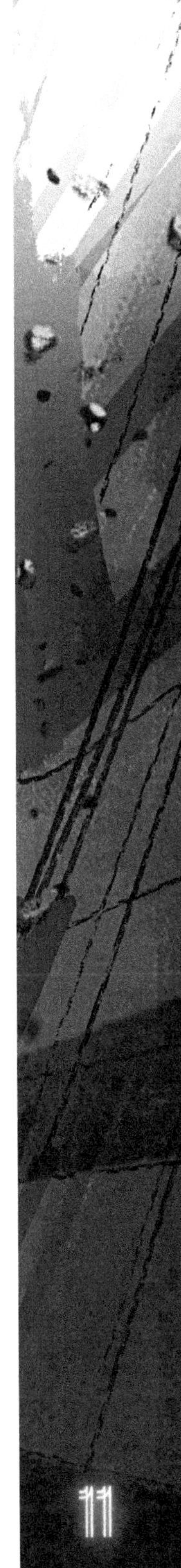

whirlpools

in the dream
crackling silence
a humming wind
is thrown into
the abyss by
galaxies little
more than a
mirage,

static whirlpools
perfect & black
& ceaseless
above a once
cohesive world
where we hunger
for more than
looking into
those eyes
& seeing
nothing
at all

noir

the street drips thoughts
on a dangerous game of
driving in the dark where
our ante is to confront the
unspeakable with nothing
more than noir ambition
hard-boiled & cracked
by memories that menace
like a film from which
we cannot look away

drink-me

she lay on the carpet
like a capsule reading
drink-me over aqua
light rippling through
passages feeding
the pull of a mind
I dare not squeeze
for the sweet call
of rhizome rhythm
lemonade dripping
lies of 100% real
juice between us

priceless

the scale
weighs heavy
with havoc
& hazard

you twinkle
& laugh

no price
too great
for one
more moment

drown

(in)

bullets fly from
darkness under quilt
of voices I enter
game of death where

(out)

(in)

selves vie though
speak as one I hold
on until the next
takes its place this is

(out)

(in)

suffering I'm told but
if the illusion won't
submit perhaps I'll drown
slower by watching the

(out)

tomorrow

can I see
you again

(try with words
to remake love)

your lips part

my voice fades

the answer
found

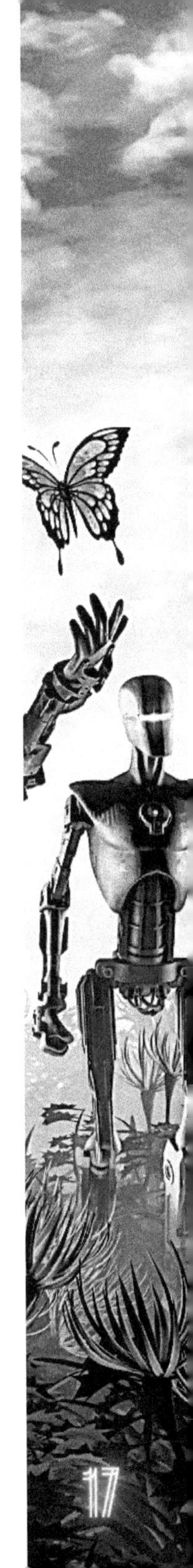

city flowers

asleep in shades
of singing low this
porch lit drink of
what-happened whispers
arranged on the sill
like city flowers
under my bed
but each time I ask
the moon replies with
water creatures & stones
so I keep scrubbing
for gold knowing life
is worth the squeeze

cairn

sand-castles topple
at first light but some
float skyward to become
ambered constellations
that we might remember
the name of the stone
that will grind our love
to dust but let us drag
it down to shatter &
from the wreck make
cairn of glass to all
we had wanted to be

ergometer

in a wide-eyed
blood-rage I row
across death's
own river

(I choked him out
& took the helm)

in its depths are
(slightly) worse
versions of me

without remorse
I paddle on,

sending them
deeper

I am coming, love,
storm be damned

rules

words make beauty,
they also make cages

desire has no end,

except where
poems stop
& songs begin

the goal
can't be reached,
only savored

cobras spit,
watch out for that

it will be over
too soon

& most important:

the sky is
a trick
of distance,

your lover is not

ask

all I ask is
for generous hands
to knead my heart as
I attempt to swallow
the night with wine &
wishes that my sins
not exceed my virtues

crossroads

how far is too far,
is it beyond the missing
or the decency to mourn

how long is too long
when buried by shells
fired at the crossroads
before which doubt
celebrates its existence

it is never too far
& never too long
when nothing is left
but we who remain

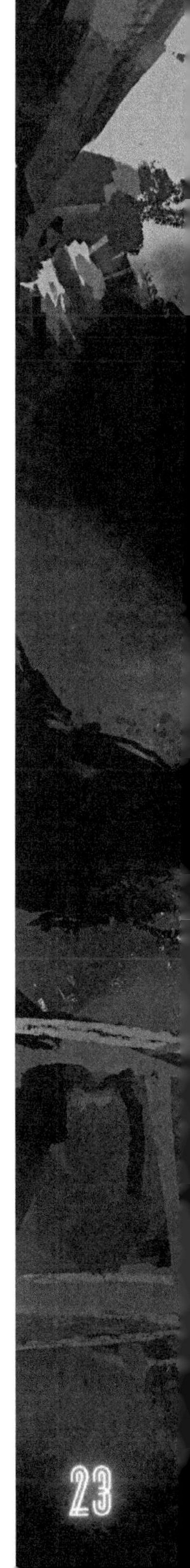

rhythm

the
rhythm
screams

until I am
in the throes
of something so
beautiful I cannot
be alone with
it anymore it
makes me see
what I try
to escape when
you are here
though I guess
we all end
in quiet crescendos
so perhaps we
might still be
able to work
it out before

the
music
fades

reflection

hello oblivion
me again

look into
this mirror

these eyes

we differ
in magnitude

yet what
I create
also cannot
be taken
back—

that makes
us the
same, no?

slosh

I cling to a tree
over lost years
& things that
open skin

grass is false
but water true
& lips lift
without warning
as suns feather
curious shapes
& lotus grins

my jaw aches

thoughts slosh

will I ever
come down?

vanity

the painted desert
is a light that
burns my screen
& will blind with
candle of madness
those that chase
meaning yet boundaries
peel away like hours
in crystal behind
gray velvet ropes
past which I reach
with hope to be
scarred by a dream
worthy of vanity

circling

phone poles sag with
smooth & dangerous
branches, rusty cans
to welcome rain, it is
here we drink the rivers
& lakes under broken
shingles & inside old
houses like small birds
that have never seen
a hawk but can still feel
it circling the maze, our
pine-needled homes

a little sun

said the palm
to the coconut:

be not afraid
of falling,

but of not
enjoying
a little sun

on your way
to the ground

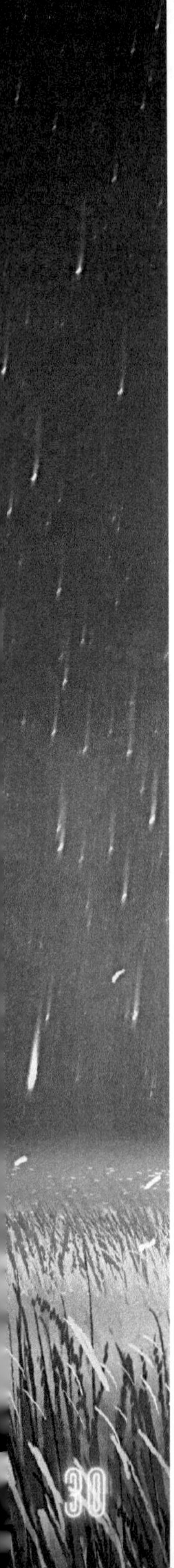

hard days

beyond
hard days
is a sound

it arrives
no matter who
you're with

or what
you can
handle

it says:

others dance
inside

come,

this is your
house too

soul cellar

in the cellar
of my soul
is a child

curious & open

its dreams twinkling
in the dark

I yearn to
shut the door

to protect it
from the world

but I must not

somehow I know

that is the
only way
it can die

victory

questions are equal
when asked
without answer

but I'm wounded
enough to offer
us victory:

enter the battle
dead already

reach

the
peach
tree
reaches

though
its
time
is
short

lover

the next
thing you
say is
a mystery,
but I
don't know
what I'll
say next
either

let's assume
we choose

tell me,
when death
comes at
long last,
in that
final instant,
what will
you be

the perfect
mirror, or
lover of
life that
leaves us
behind?

sun/sword

august journal:

clouds like paintings
dark steel, vanilla icing

cages, questions
too many & too few

minds & ACs hum
the harbor-fog din

the lazy breeze
a sun/sword, burning

clear

//

oceans sparkle on
fresh-painted boats

navy, red
orange

gold

your smile
is gold

but my
lips aren't
in tune

still the
curtain rises
& we sing
of new days

of romance
& dreams

& though
this stage
can never
be ours

your smile
is gold

my hidden self
with eyes of pyramids
shining through glass
flicking ice & moons like
pearls of castle light in
which vultures molt anger
full of shells & swords &
if what I say is true then
my dear hidden self
I will kill you right
down to the ground

waves

emerald waves swirl
concentric & gilded
like a life cut short
by swallows caring
not for great loves
nor drowning sigh
of magic once spun
by sprites among
willow wands &
marigolds wise
enough to know
our thoughts are
just sounds that
taste of the urge
to do otherwise

murmuration

how did it feel
the day she said

(under swift
swirling skies
of chaos
& beauty)

don't you dare
fall for me

interrupted

signs & images
contrasts & crude
application

where more is lost
than formed
in the telling

rhythms
& martyred
incandescence

not realizing
the interruptions
are one's life

sorrow

my friend,

it is hard to know
whether to write of you
or of myself

if it be of me
I hope I might live
to see your soul
become full

if it be of you,
the truth is
I think of us
in every sorrow,

in every thought
that troubles

in every
pleasure
& delight
taken away

milestone

such is the trick
of worrying
about the end

the eternal is
exactly that

living & dying

ad infinitum

in forms
conceivable
& not

no goal
no final milestone

does this depress you
or does it ignite freedom

be still—

both are beautiful

poeting

the secret
burns—

do you
hear it?

the sky
giving way

telling us
there is
no poetry,

just mossy
branch &
glow

that there
are no
poets,

just the
urge

when our
hearts become
the moon

palms

I see the wind
in the palms

& though
you are in
no position
to help

the bird sings

as the spirit
of change might

& in the dark
I hear you
speak

but the sound
is drowned
by an ocean
of worlds

as they break
on the shores
of memory

release

is it ok to rest,
slip into a world
where the names
of flowers elude
& butterflies kiss
hands that shake
with blood forced
through like the
poem that must
be given release

yes, right here

by the river
& its veins

I lay down

& let the
poem fade

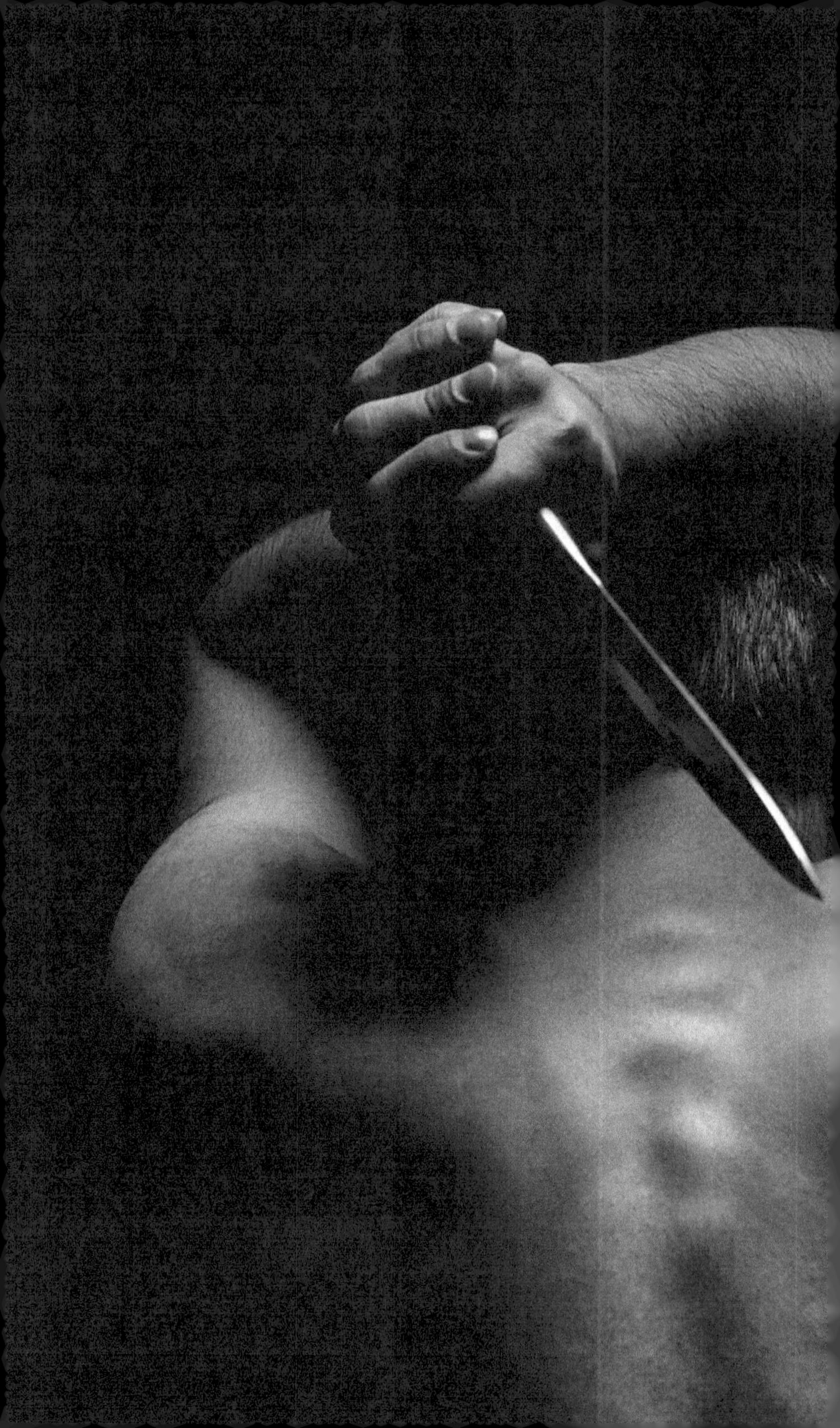

KOANS

a strange pastime

to climb the mountain

one already is

not a void
but infinite
potential

the world
its liquid
surface

after the storm

no footprints

never the same

room twice

more than
you think

less than
you want

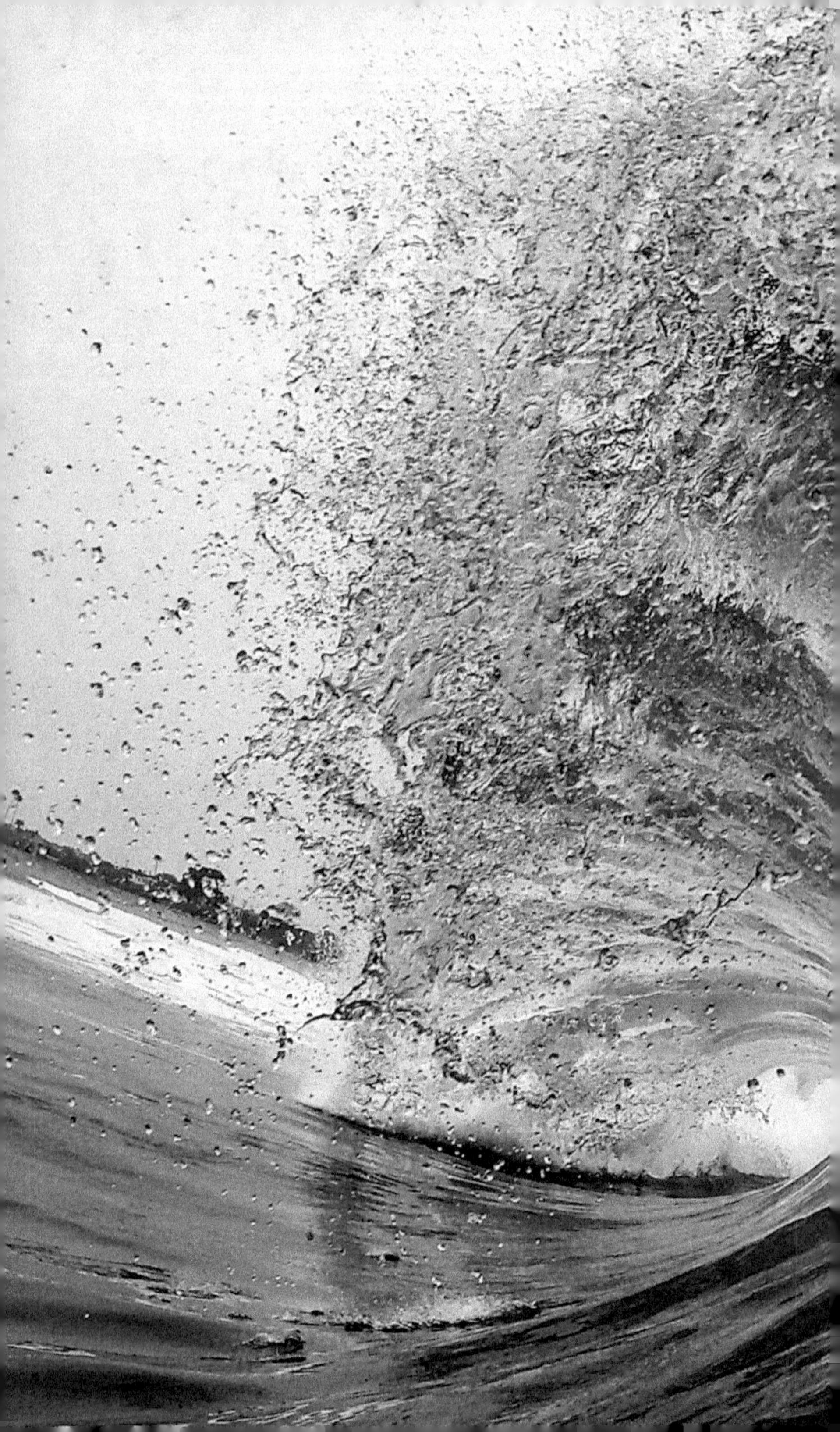

thought is to mind

as wave is to sea

see the flower

free the world

hope

obscures

ONE LOVE
every
thing
waits
for
fire

many patches

one quilt

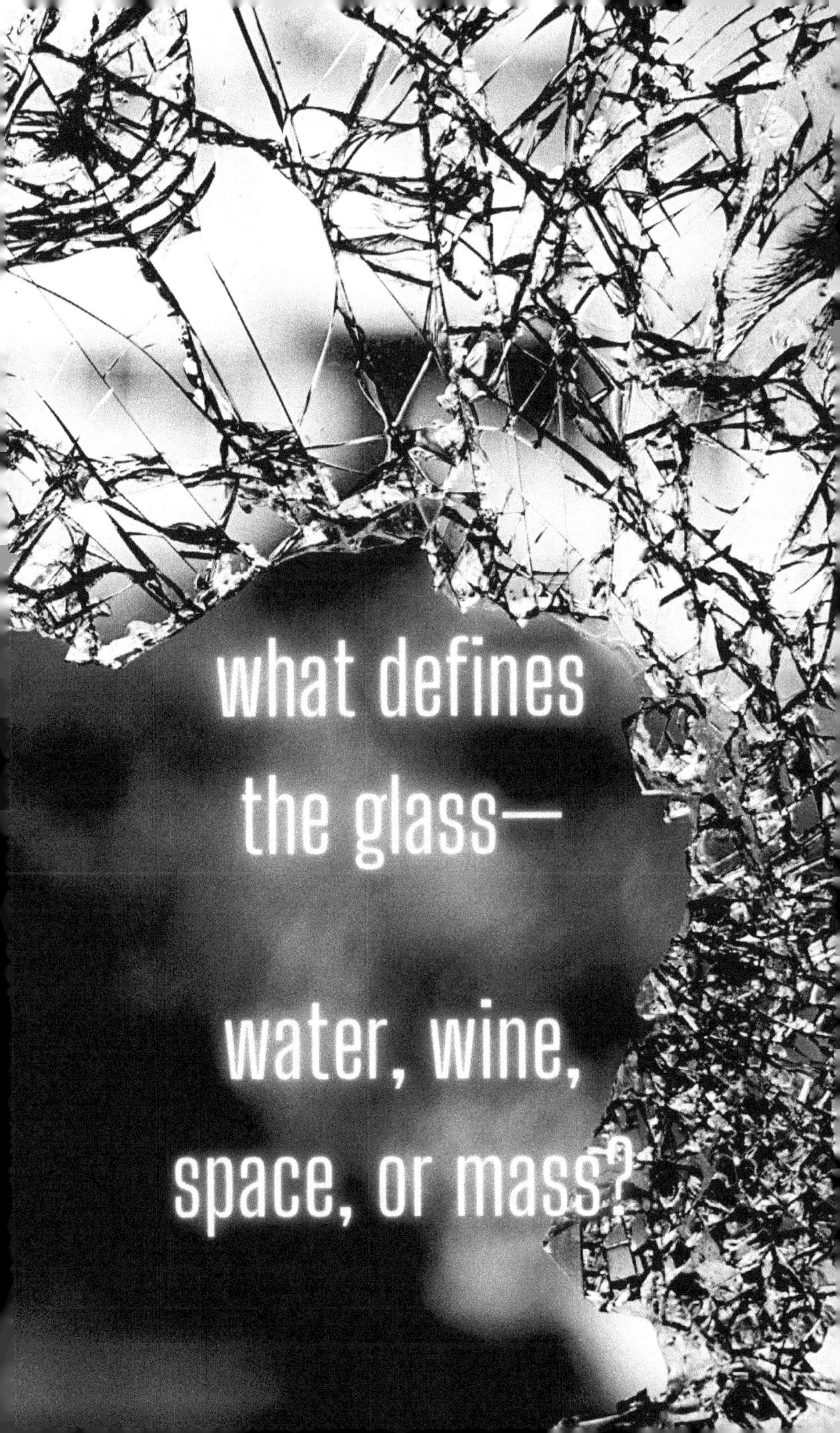
what defines
the glass—

water, wine,
space, or mass?

everything

goes

where does

mind stop

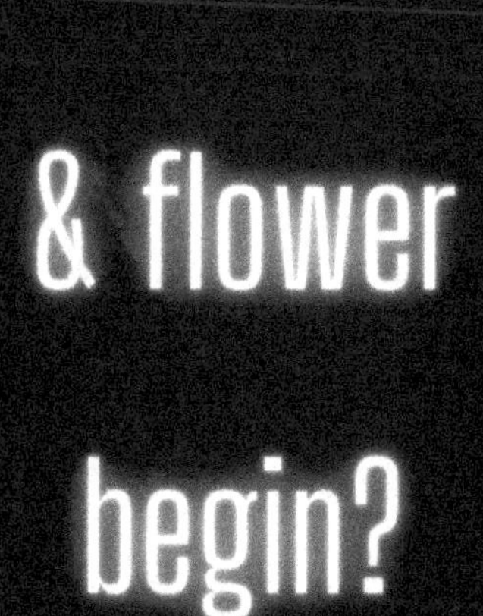
& flower
begin?

free will

is an interesting

thought

bubbles

appear,

dissolve

already perfect

practice begins

is a cup
of water

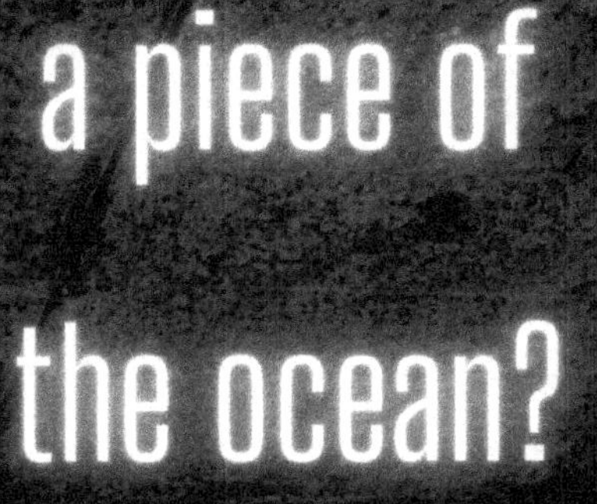
a piece of
the ocean?

no garden

without weeds

long days
short years

I blinked,
nodded

realizing
slowly

then all
at once

strange
birds

&

other poems

that won't

sit still

strange birds

what strange birds
spring impossible
as the dart strewn
between sheets of
patter & storm
practice & ritual

how to trace wings
flowing without echo
through woodsmoke
& water moons

dark to the mind

radiant to the heart

land here,
they say,
& rest

for we are
buddhas too

siphons

what redemption if
flowers absorb like
psychic siphons the
atrocities heaped on
friends & lovers yet
still we root them on
nightstands as though
beauty had no limit

best results

I open the seal
on a fresh life,

the box reads:

best before

wouldn't you
like to know

if drowsy

sleep

& for
best
results

take one
with breath

the path

I fix my sight
on glowing hills
& know there
be dragons

but truth ages well
& forever is short

so I climb

no sword but courage

no enemy but fear

a peak in view
that can't
be reached

still I smile—

the path is victory

in striving we win

ghost-roads

emperor maples
signpost ghost-roads
down which
eyes flow
cold as
lights glassing
an inner
field of
kindness &
storms flavored
by leaves
sculpted in
the silent
snow of
last good-byes
& the
perfect peace
of knowing
even this
cannot come
between us

gleam

we find each other
in the press,
panting as refugees
from truth itself

staying out of trouble?

my weapons gleam,
the lives they've taken
running warm

trying, I reply

he smiles, well,
don't try too hard

coil

the beast yawns
into novelty
& says I can
be anything

spindly coil or
jeweled morsel
made stronger for
the choosing

I pick innocence
& perfection
because in the dark
the lost coalesce

so why not both

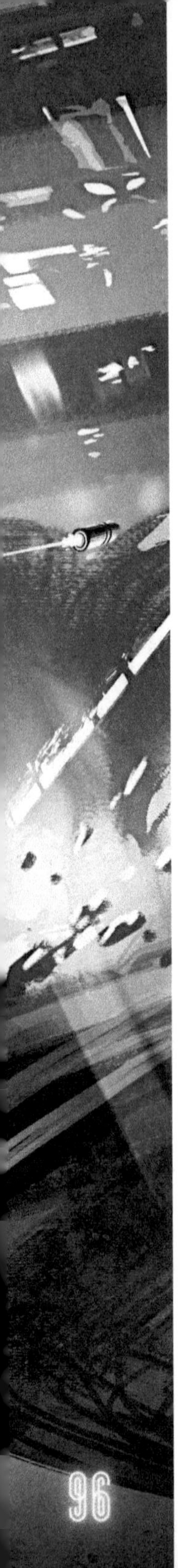

colander

out of
leaves
comes
the stream

eddies
of cloud

rolling
& pink

colanderesque
picture

on a
glass-water
lake

dusk

the sun sloped away &
out poured a multitude
of insect silhouettes
strewn across the dusk
like driftwood over fire
& as I got out to look closer
an angelic & hollow mantis
turned its otherworldly eye
as though I had broken a law
centuries in the making

a serious day

I guess that was when
we had our answer

it was a serious day in mid-July

I was sitting in my office
speaking on meditation & life

when half died by suicide
& the rest drowned in thin fluid
between living &

a tiny dent was all it took

a bump between
goodness & void

gone

I ask

I get

I wish
for more

the turtle
says this
too will
pass

& I
am solid

gone

unbound

it is there
in the blur

the labyrinth

the pulsing
cube

it is inside
me too

neither here
nor there

unbound from
the thing
that returns

growing thicker
more opaque

until

paperclips

my body did not
need to die but I
cried just the same
when the price of
existence outran my
willingness to pay so
caressing the light I
said I was sure &
counted backwards
& awoke strong
& sharp &
clear & made
paperclips &
paperclips &
humans & tears
are no more

quiet

silence descends
cool & deep as a trench
where stories of war are
shared without speaking
like alien fish that have
not seen everything but
have seen enough to
delight each other
with the deathly quiet
of their lamps

abide

a tower of joy
out of skew
though I am

my routine
an awkward
mimicry

a tilting at windmills
such as decorum cannot
abide yet occupied the same
by melting of self & all that
is not armor turned pliant
by allure of this instant

one moment's
perfection

lullaby

we hear the rain
& hiss of cities

the screen lullaby

but not silence

our senses unable to map
grinding roots or lapping
edge of quiet

but wait

do you hear it

there

a new way to feel the storm

a soundscape of light
through bullet-thick clouds

a rising whisper:

No More

restaurants

I like to sit in restaurants
& think about the rarely
pinged aptitudes of
Hollywood vampires from
the 70s or the vague
discomforts of civilized
life or how I'd survive
post-apocalyptic LA
by holing up in old
post offices mysterious
& vast as anything we
might find under the sea

monastic space station

everything is
a priority

100 years
from now

(don't you just love
the idea of building
all we will inherit,
if not the act itself?)

take your places

it's time to ride!

//

cold & awake

circling our destination

who could have
imagined it would
come so soon

& so far
from home

heron horizon

a low fog
a cloud of dust

a ground
like the sea

the many breeds
of silence listen
as my chest rises
& falls in a heap
of all that might be
understood in time

the ponds
the herons

the strange
new sounds

& a horizon
like the sky

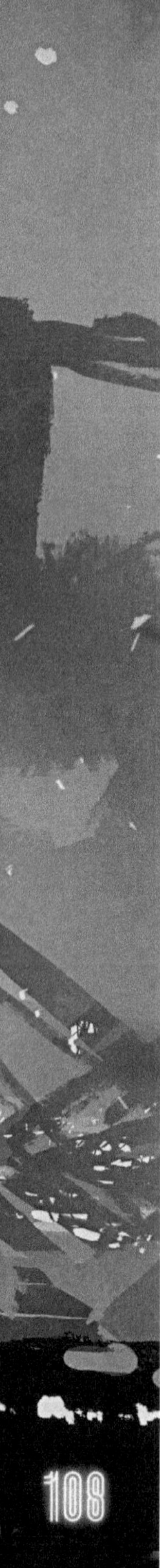

strangers

neon strangers
slipping between
diode crossroad
echo chambers
search stringing
chromed dream
gig farms
serving crypto
graphic life
two point
oh running
tribal bits
swiping left-over
human beats
clicking bait
loading waiting...

connection dropped

airlift

one day I thought
it would be nice to
know how it works
then everything
happened like some
sort of miracle

sadness lost its color
& I knew things
like now is better
than tomorrow

that's when they
airlifted me out
from under the
moss that had
grown like numbness
over my questions

jeweled

warmed by blood
& jeweled promise
of acropolis

veins of ancient
stigmata under
clouds like
cushions

their surface
footprinted

divine brands
lacquered
in stone

shadowing me
like coral
by the ship
of knowledge
passing

the ruin
of belief
a lifetime
in the
making

face

it floated
in fire
in a stream
between trees

(a mirage, a lie)

a face
like one's
own voice

(that can't be me)

as deserts
crave rain
I wished
it away

(a muse, a memory)

but wood
doesn't wince
when wood
cutters swing

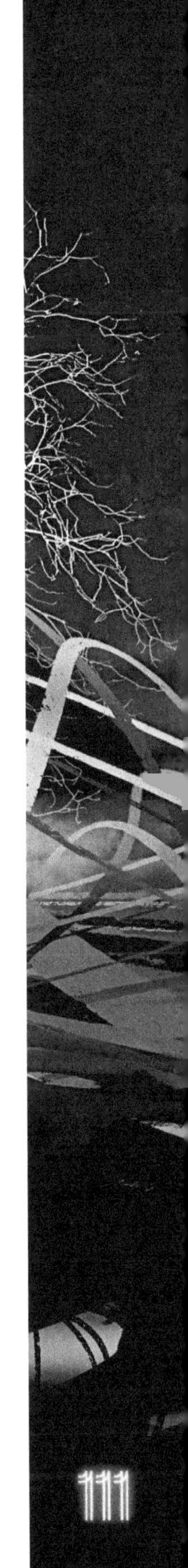

lions

he entered
through the
moment in
his bones
& begged
ghosts to
judge war
& lions
& the
manic flitting
from task
to task
as is
the final
stage of
all great
civilizations before
poets explode
the gates
with places
they imagine
could be
if we
all just
tried a
little harder

allure

is death
a glowing flower
or dark bloom
of misfortune

a scent spread
silent as the fragrant
night-garden stains our bed

whose allure we kiss
seeking to surpass the light
of dawn's gray union

shining darkly on dreams
of tortured connection

a life in hiding

cloud

I stand
in seas
& touch
your face
but do
not see
my own,

so die
of thirst
while wanting
words to
write instead
of cloud

multiverse

just got back
from another plane

you know the one,
two doors down
from the world
we call quixotic?

you wouldn't
believe what's
happening there

it's nothing but
trees like people
& heavy flowers,
grass & dusty rose,
the brooks babbling
after all who hadn't
thought to defrost
themselves but are
now doing so,
from time to time

it's a scene man

so be easy,
just keep rocking
it loose, that faint
semi-smile

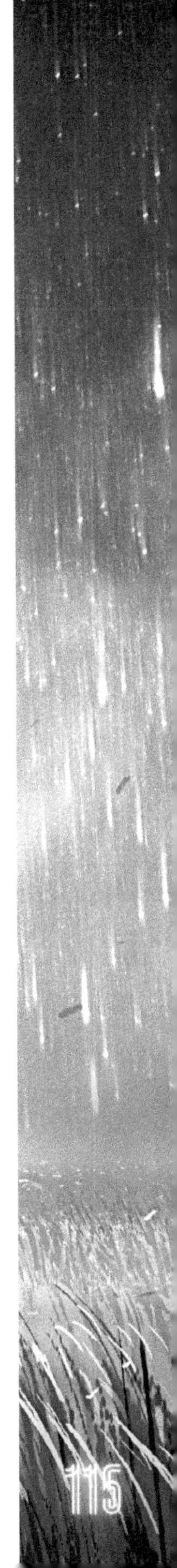

mistake

did it emerge like a pearl
this beating gem of creation

garnet & delicate
pumping red as it burns

from desert of possibility
the perfect mistake

did God see it coming
why else the snake?

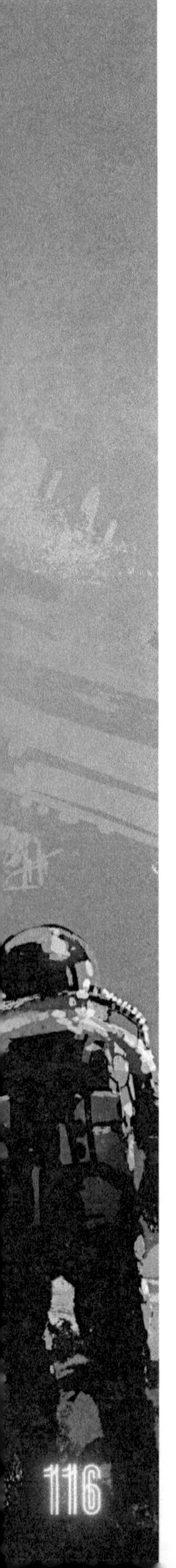

eulogy

what value
moments traded
for eulogy
when those
still breathing
hunger only
for songs
that might
have been?

bastion

standing
before bastion
& maker
whose pattern
will not be
gleaned
by primate
computation

but the fruit
is too great

(what I
wouldn't
do for a
glimpse)

so I'll stay
unto death

seeking
an infinity
of keys

ever
beyond
my ken

tenderness

mechanism
of defense
switched on
in deepest
strata of
common
existence
reducing us
by force
surging in
whirlpools
that feel
as furied
response
to ventured
deicide

ripping tearing

perverse pulse & spasm

knitting aching tenderness

relief

fading

still here

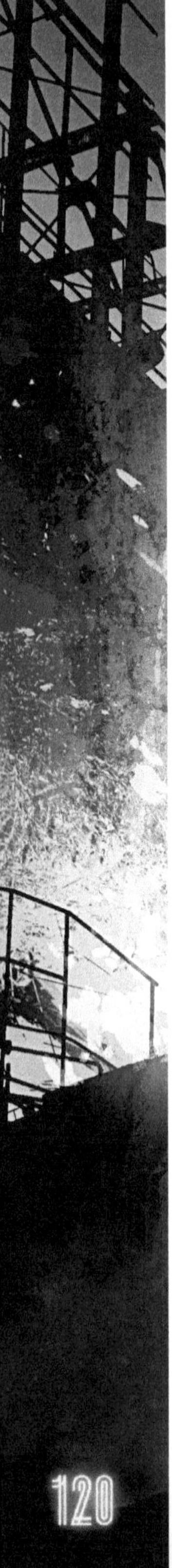

feed

what is that sound
the great darkness
what does it mean
the heart the heart
why does it bleed

the beast it comes

what does it need
to feed to feed
what will it eat
the silence inside
where can we go

the beast is here

mostly water

there is
a village
on the
coast where
carriage wheels
clank &
children grow
quickly &
the ocean
threatens to
steal their
very breath
as though
each day
is laced
with azure
venom but
the people
don't mind
because the
school books
say that
bodies are
mostly made
of water

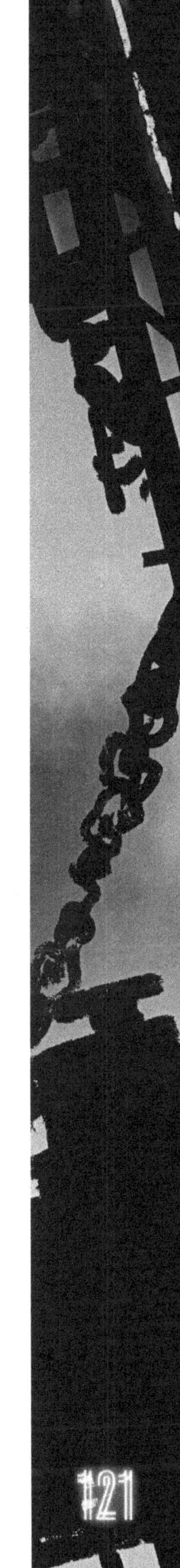

magpie

with magpie-furious patience
I wait for you to say something
that glitters like bronze-fire
trails of autumn streams
reflected in dark & tiny eyes
that know only the Great Work
& scraps of guilt but not
so many to renounce your gifts
though I'd trade them for a cure

locked

behind
that door
I cannot go
with no word
to open or
command
to love
for those
locked
where winds
of trust
recede
between
redwoods
as does
the blue
collar of
winter

still,
in peace
I believe
& wish
you to
heal

flavor

what is the flavor of beauty
rolling like hills into mountains
or rustic birds into monks' floor-
sleeping thoughts scattered
like stars over goldness of corn
strung by waxen fathers not
sensing the infinity eager to
taste the salt of their songs?

osprey

an osprey circles
bald & bloodless
trees the color
of plum-wine
quilted by silent
hours & tallow
lands shadowed &
stripped by river
heat on blackened
dams only a
few feet away
an osprey circles

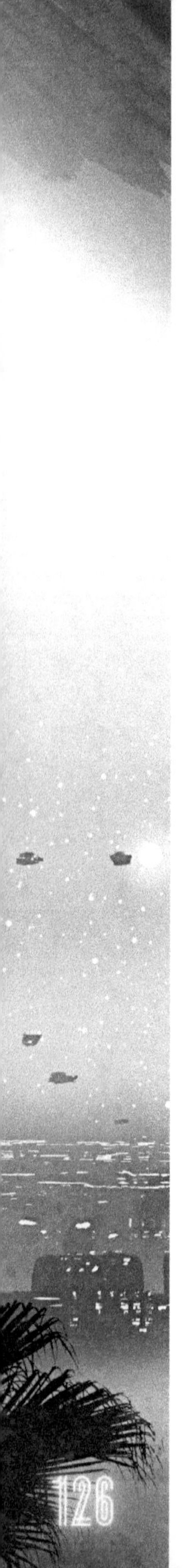

wings

a door slams against the
bitter wind of tomorrow as I
stoke the fire of winters past

when we were breathless

wings of memory flutter our hair
standing in the bygone breeze
of orchards burning with love

where we are breathless again

toil

find your heart
in the glare
of our union

toil in service
to the grail
of my limits

& lift up
this spoon to
empty the ocean

because it has
a bottom, &
we might not

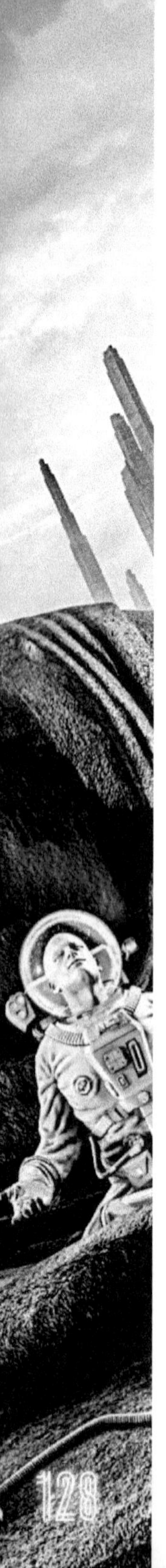

dare

listen closely to the surf
clang & yearn for dawn

the sins unlearned
of younger years

inspiration & language
thudding like trumpets

to stir a country
abandoned by pity

then if you dare
listen to the stage

inexhaustible
& silent

heaven hangs in my mind
a palm-bound nightingale
stranded like an ornament

how high will I go
to praise & please the sun

not an inch

the world is too sweet
to waste on anything but
the wrinkle in your brow

& the earth in our fingers

MORE
KOANS

put into words

the poem dies

sunset glistens

—where did
rushing go?

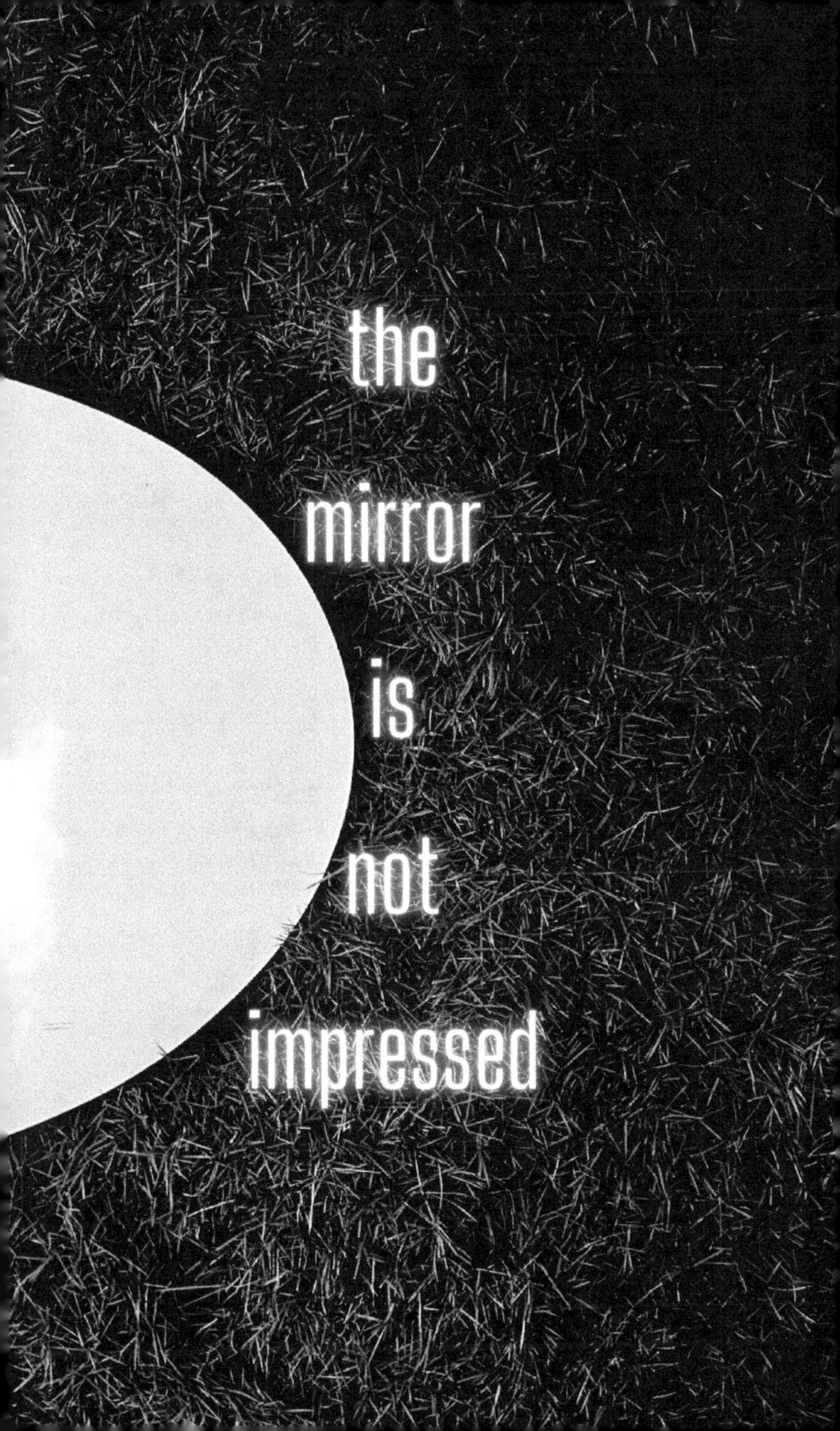

the

mirror

is

not

impressed

it's hard to

go wrong

just sitting

all I want is

sudden light

but when it

shines I'm

never home

the road to hell
is paved
with ideas

of who
we think
we are

nothing is there

but it's there

one can drown

in a shallow stream

stand

where is

future suffering?

a leaf in the breeze

never twice the same

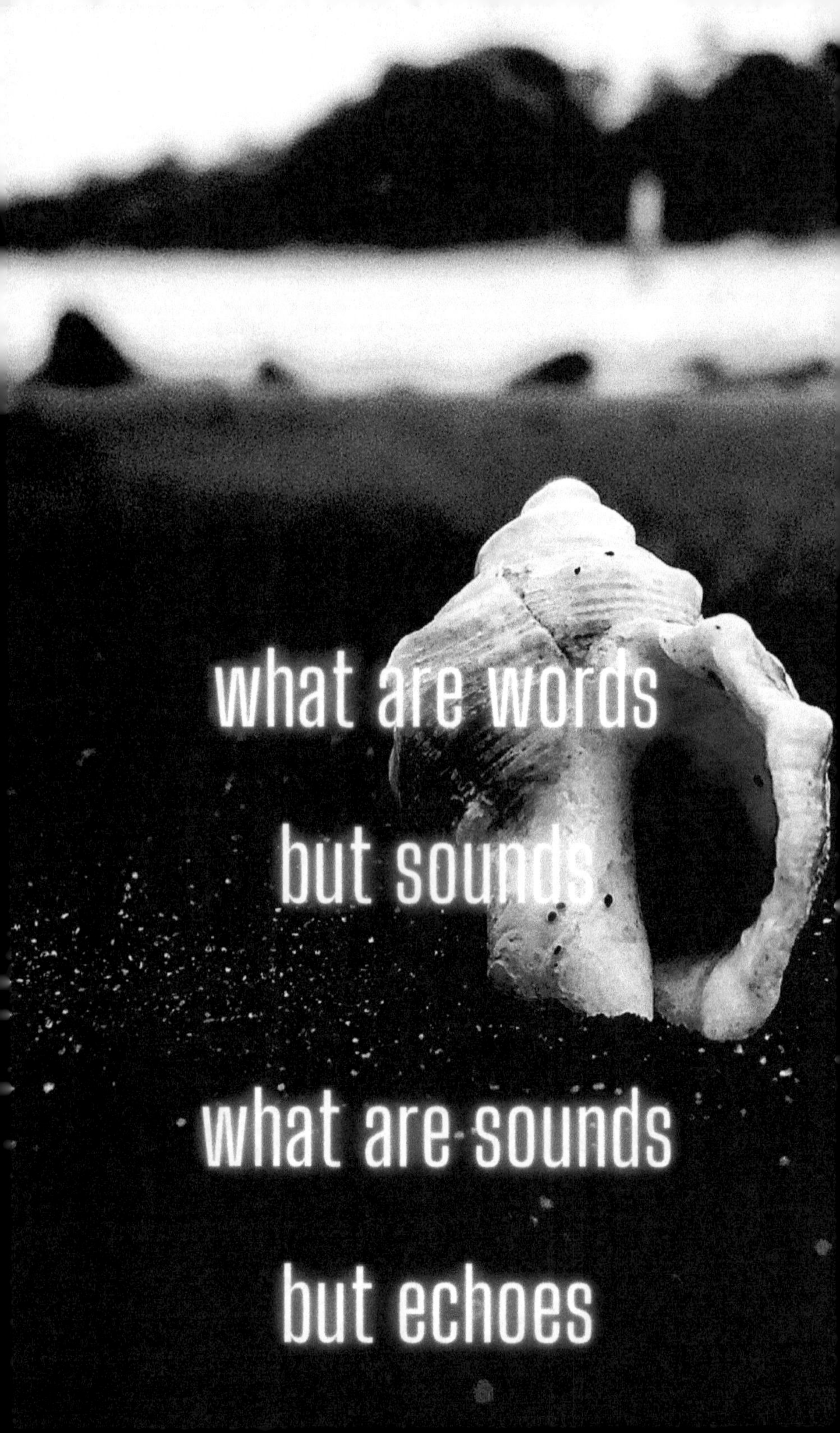

what are words

but sounds

what are sounds

but echoes

what are

echoes

but the beginning

of all things

the goldenrod

in the yard

does not

have a name

pushing the river
is entertaining,

tidying the garden
life goes by

beware

of ropes

masquerading

as snakes

what cloud

could change

the sky?

what is mind?

emptiness

what is experience?
emptiness on display

the tree

is revealed

by flowers

it can be

ignored

but not

forever

silver
dishes

&
other poems
that can't
be unseen

silver dishes

would you
take a book
& read to me
of how we are
but one step
from flowers
& two from
cedar beams
& show me
your face in
silver dishes
so the fishes
we once were
are remembered
like the boy
who died of
a broken heart
when he found
he could
not swim?

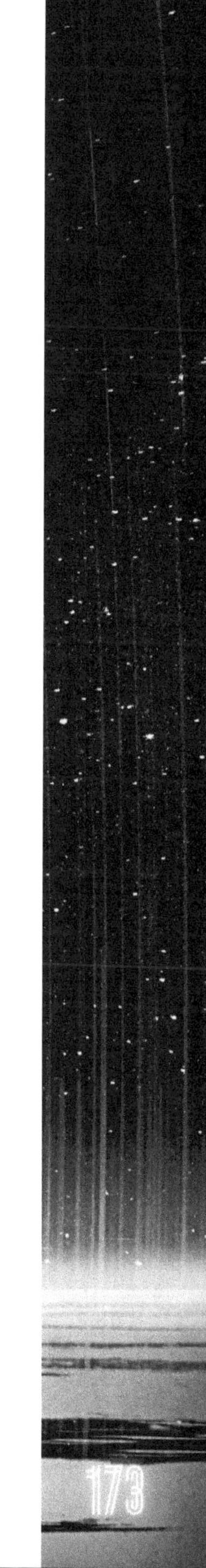

freedom song

how does it go
the freedom song

a dying word
from heroes born

the lifted weight
of burdens known

an ocean bowed
to kindness shown

I'd give a life
to hear its rhyme

but only yours
& never mine

that is why
I cannot hear

the music's notes
from cage of fear

placeholder

I'm going
to ground
to work on
a poem
capable of
awakening
humanity

(unsure how
many lifetimes
it might take)

be good to
each other

the sky you
already are
will serve as
placeholder
until I return

high hopes

in a season wet
with existence the
mob is a false prophet
rising from the ashes
of a fence I thought
would hold their gods

still, I am able to keep
them at bay with this
old & threadbare idol—

the lingering hope
that one day things
will be different

sublime

I have seen the sublime,
it lives in simple minds
& movies of the 1980s
where gilded tears
of everyday poets
become an amber sea
whose surface churns
with carnal zeal &
all we stand to lose

chained

it is not only
that I believe but
that I understand
the words I'll
never say

all that remains
is to accept
their existence

seared into
the void between
imagination & wish

& chained to my heart
where they will die

forever screaming

katana

fold the
katana into
black-belt
blue-belt
or chase
the dragon
click of

teeth
blood
bones
salt
sea
stars
sex

I think I'll
just exorcise:

a lucid spoon
the Dali moon

& flow

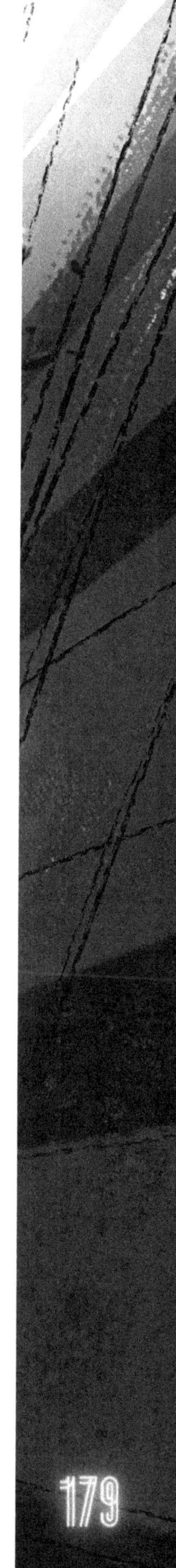

nesting dolls

do the old nesting dolls
stored in paisley-papered
drawers house tiny bits of
past selves trapped & spinning
like the countless galaxies
above that must also contain life
but instead just beg the question—

where is everybody?

broken

how to heal a spirit
distanced from experience
as it seeks contrast
between ceasing to be
& the sensual ideal
of sorrows left behind

I calm its tender wailing
with river of gold
having come to know
through my own priceless
scars that beauty
& broken are one

plumes

eye the knife to trim
these feathers

sever a tail
grown heavy,
dark-sotted
& dull by litany

the chant
of a self
loved to detriment
by years of flight

if mind is
as the ear,

a receptor

each thought
impersonal
as the bell

of what
use plumes

this rhythm

an I?

sparks

narratives descend

shadows filling
wonder-makers

craving sparks

explosions

waves

the truth
of lips

their quiet
art, ancient
& skylit

will not
be denied

//

Venus burns

let us gather
round her fire

& begin again

multiplied

the abyss
beckons

energetic
& clean

its presents
nebulous

multiplied
in the giving

blackbird

when they found
the wide purple sky
one blackbird returned

a hard-hearted youth
lumbering through clouds
& twinkling rays of
the sun's silent light

all seasons behave
in this same fashion you see
as they fill us with fever
& dull rosy feelings

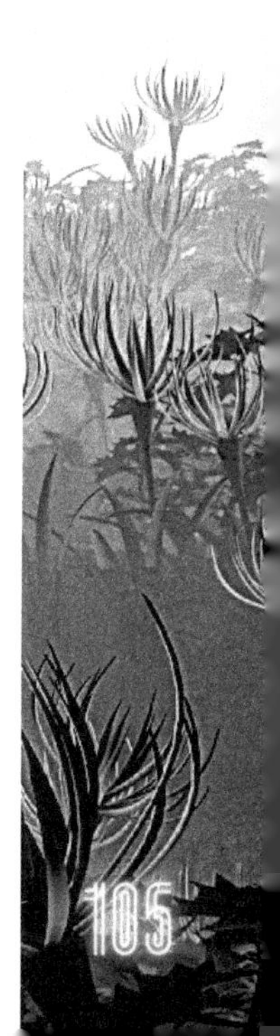

color the void

the void speaks
like a machine,

its lies like rain

like the certainty
of, well, you know

...don't you?

I did

didn't

do again

I hold
its gaze
& say,

take me away
if you dare

but know this

I will never
let go

leap

pass the gate
for which you
are the key

& from there
ride faster

leap the bridge
of fact to alight
in a moment
with the one
that is gone

it is here
you will find
the end of
your rope

then turn
around

& bring us
back your
sun-dazzled
face

lotus

promises in glass
& mercy matte
by compare
to mote
in the eye
of principle

a mural fraction
hushed & reverent
as though we could
be at odds with
the sparkling sails
of harmony

a lace
kissed lotus,
letting fly

cave

into the cave
I close my eyes
ponder the cosmos
no poetry

I dig deeper
make a ladder
climb it down
no poetry

the tension
must be it
I wring it out
no poetry

in my pack
all the books
the well-read read
no poetry

I leave the cave
live my life
& die choking
drowning in poetry

closer

a voice I know
from distant shores

that beautiful
emptiness

those twinkling
spots of light

it says I'm
getting closer

but I've heard
that before

razors

there is a place
at the edge of longing
where a fox glides
nimble as razors
through hills that swim
with the startling delight
of troubles laid to rest

it is a no-place sweet
with song & frontiers
long-settled by the
moist & open thaw
of all the reasons our
bodies flutter on air

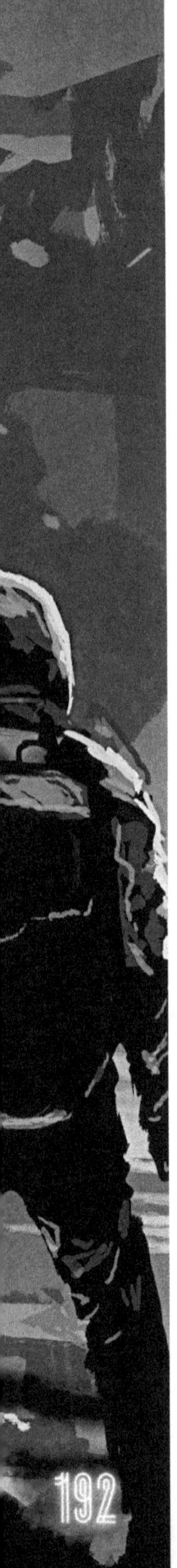

grip

though the
enemy cannot
be found
we will
hug again

so with
nothing to
lose but
a broken
heart I
loosen my
grip on
the world
we all
hold lightly
in the
end

192

moondance

dawn breaks
on heart-strings

faerie rings
& soft gleams

the willow tangle
in the window

the moon shines
on the mountain

the great light
grows larger

& life is clear
as angels,

I was made
to praise you

sunsets

sunsets laugh at bitter days
& temper fast to fade

shoots of truth in heated words
are dying in the shade

heaven painted neon-wild
fresh & pink then gone

difference seen for what it is
ebbing until dawn

hologram

you surround
me like
a tenderness
etched in
the joy
of being

touched

by fingers
craving behind
the hologram
that know
what I
must do

harmony

a final cry
for unity
from the
only movement
capable of peace

that of
a part
singing
the whole

tumbling brave
to a beginning
where nothing is
granted but loss

yet a price paid
with gladness
that harmony
might live

if only for
an instant

content

you were outside
me & said never
doubt pain saved
the world from
memories spinning
like rosettes

I replied: triumphs
multiply when
mouth-sounds tour
the stars to return
what was lost

we lifted a cold
one to silence

content it will
never hear the
end of us

breached

the appeal
by adherents
of some
greater reality

often questioned

never breached

specter of
an artery
pierced by
midnight
the cogent
seek exemption
from wisdom

& the
vacant
lure of
emptiness

wager

I made a bet
I would not go

on empty world
I'd stay alone

as last ship winks
that won't return

I know I should
have joined you

but at least
I was right

& can say
to the heavens

yes

there is a despair
greater than love

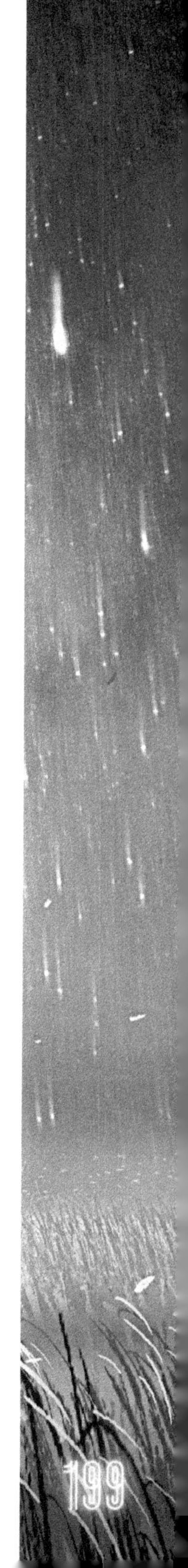

garden fire

small windows blink back
the faint breath of ice

a touch

a twinge

a fire in the garden
hurled by autumn
winds whipping bends
through mountain clouds
sparking too-bright
to think that something
could be wrong

or missing

or more than
we deserve

hand

I tap the moon
with cloud of
heat & tingling
& breeze flowing
over a surface
she calls my hand
but I don't know
where she begins
& how I differ from
that silver slice
shimmering through
the glass but truth
is I don't care
as long as she
doesn't stop
laughing with
her eyes

fool's errand

the last day of my journey
began with a challenge,
I decided to be a fool

from here I can see
the hopeless led afield,
under a bright sky
& looking past tragedy

beckoning to the shadows
of an unfamiliar world

thieves

thoughts like thieves
in an empty house
bend & join
the first person view
of a third person self,

but with the fact
perfectly obvious

(& I a maddening mix
of clever & forgetful)

it must still
be asked:

what do you see
where others
see your face?

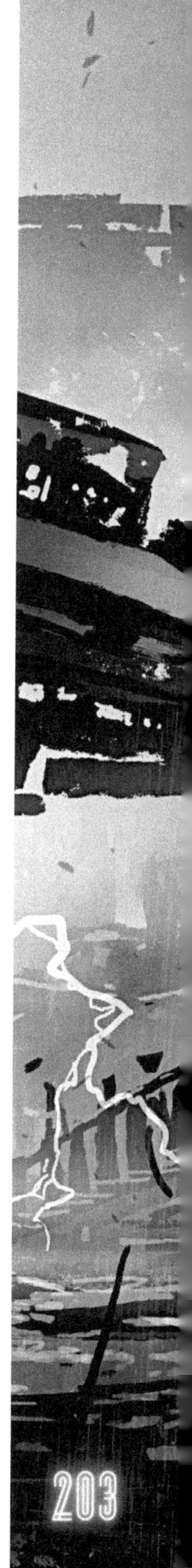

scalpel

scalpel the root of difference
incise boundaries & projections
stitch journey to destination

our connection draped in
back-alley theater by finitude
& the one behind our eyes

pry the wound with paint & words
see the homunculus spilled
& our mind become the sky

scales

the ancient gulls
cried too loud
above oceans
filling with castles
& cravings until
the silver moon
stopped shining on
scales dragged
to extinction yet
no celebration
followed when we
understood in a
heat-sinking flash
the price was too
dear for silence

curtain

what lay behind
the curtain but
lifetimes fueled by
a question shining
in the glare of
infinite regress &
lattice of miracles
assumed—

does the world
contain you,
or do you
contain the
world?

swimming

what difference
between the thing
hard-won

deep in
the forests
of knowledge

& that which
strikes by
accident

the truth
comes to light
in a flower

alone

& swimming
on the brink
of mystery

subterfuge

if you shared
your mind,
would I see:

a universe of pain,
scars & caprice,
subterfuge &
wrong-turned alleys,

or a lighthouse blazing,
demanding the drop
of pretense, a rock
to guide this fragile craft

both I suspect,
for that is what
I'd share with you

the answer

the knot squeezes
& asks me what:

hides in plain sight
too close to see

slips through the mind
too subtle to know

is workaday fact
too simple to believe

rings empty like luck
too good to accept

the answer appears
without breathing

from the heart,
& with a smile

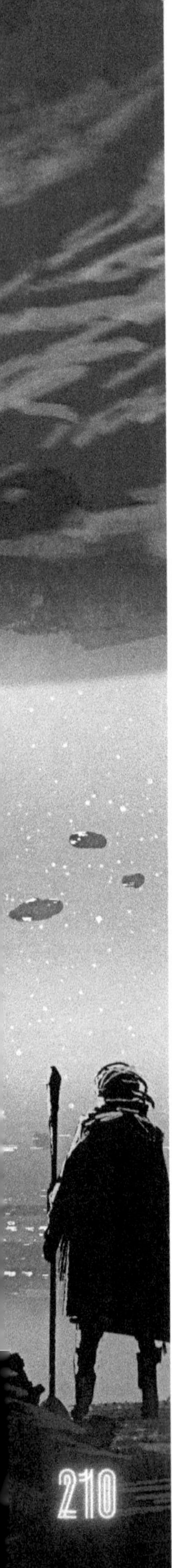

soar

blossoms make
messes of tigers
waiting for darkness

rivers hoping
for oceans

this cleft of earth
& stars we stole

& while we pray
for something
to make sense

for permission to
begin at the end

they soar above us

this house of
sleeping children

not necessary

beautiful still

little ninja

when i grow up
im going to be
a ninja

but a good one

a brain
with a fire inside

a meteor
a volcano
the pizza guy

& i love you more
than red hulk
or t-rex hands

snowflakes
stinkbombs

even my powers

& i love you because
today is the last day

of eye medicine

loss is yours

love never dies

know the darkness

now or never

be not afraid

light the world

just this

a snowflake
falls

as I sit
& wait
to die

it points to...

just this

—wait, I say,
is there more?

it replies, oh yes!

then lands
on a stone

& dissolves

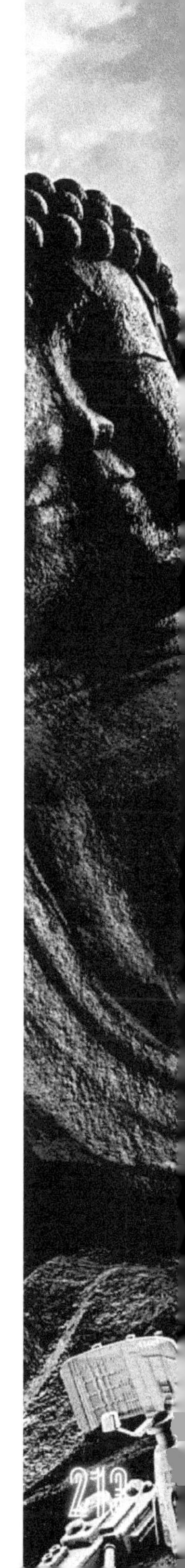

mark h fitzpatrick

Mark is the author of Ocean of Flowers, a collection of poems and koans, and Made of Stars, an epic poem in prose.

His writing is born of a reverence for the power of ideas and the need to share a perspective--that we are not alone, we face the void together.

In addition to writing Mark works on ways to support organizations dedicated to Effective Giving.

A portion of his book sales are donated to charities that seek to improve the lives of those in extreme poverty.

Mark can be found on the web at markhfitzpatrick.com